Make God A Habit
A
21-Day
Challenge

ASA PUBLISHING CORPORATION
AN INNOVATIVE OUTSOURCE BOOK PUBLISHING HYBRID

ASA Publishing Corporation
1285 N. Telegraph Rd., PMB #376, Monroe, Michigan 48162
An Accredited Publishing House with the BBB
www.asapublishingcorporation.com

Copyrights©2019 Deidre Joyner, All Rights Reserved
Book Title: Make God A Habit *A 21-Day Challenge*
Date Published: 04.12.2019 / Edition 1 *Trade Paperback*
Book ID: ASAPCID2380784
ISBN: 978-1-946746-53-5
Library of Congress Cataloging-in-Publication Data

This book was published in the United States of America.
Great State of Michigan

Table of Contents

DEDICATION

In Memory of

my grandmother *Mary Patterson* who always told me to get on my knees and pray that the good Lord take a liking to me. I thank you for being an example of a woman of faith and wisdom. I miss you so much!

and

To my only granddaughter *Gabriella*, always stand strong in The Lord!
Grandmomma Loves You!

ACKNOWLEDGEMENTS

I would like to give a special thanks to my cousin Lena Banks, The Queen of urban fiction and poetry. Thank you so much for sharing your knowledge with me for the last couple years. Your teachings and encouragement have been such a blessing. Your gift of writing is absolutely insane, and I pray that God will continue to bless your work.

I love you, Cousin

I would also like to thank my sister Kathrine Fizer, a newly established author. Thank you for leading me to ASA Publishing. Without you this moment will not be possible. May God continue to bless the work of your hands.

Love, D.

Introduction

It was the third day of a five day fast when God put it on my heart to write a book. This made no sense because at the time I was in the process of completing a different book. I had been working on that project for over two years and was excited about getting the book finished, published and in the hands of God's people. So, starting a new book was the furthest thing on my mind, this was definitely something that I had to take to God in prayer.

As I prayed, God spoke. He first gave me the title, "Make God A Habit", a couple days later it was put on my heart to add the *21-Day Challenge*. That idea came because we currently live in an era of 10 and 21-day challenges. Most of them leaning towards fitness and weight loss goals. So why not start a challenge that will get you spiritually fit, closer to God, and help you to become a better person from the inside out.

At first, it wasn't clear on how long the challenge would be, 10, 21, or 30 days. I didn't want it to be too short or too long. My heart became fixed on 21 days because it was once believed that it takes approximately 21 days to form a new habit. Some researchers say that this theory is a myth. Modeling Habit Formation in the Real World, a study conducted by Phillippa Lally in July 2009, consisted of 96 volunteers who chose an eating, drinking, or activity behavior to do daily for 12 weeks. At the end of the 12 weeks the study concluded that it takes anywhere from 18-254 days to form a new habit. One must take into consideration the determination of the person participating, and the simplicity or difficulty of the new task. The study also found that missing one day of the new behavior had no impact on the overall outcome of the individual's ability to form a new habit.

Prayer and the information in this study led me to make the decision for the 21-day challenge. So, there it was, the final title of my new book, "Make God A Habit *A 21-Day Challenge*". This book contains a daily scripture (For the purpose of understanding, some scriptures contain two versions, the second version brings the scripture to a modern context), a prayer, a declaration, and a time for self-reflection by means of a journal activity. Each day is different and contains a different message, some days will encourage you and bring you joy. Other days will bring you comfort and peace. And some days my friends; will be challenging, leading you to examine the inner most depths of your heart and soul.

To get the most of this 21-day journey with God, please take the time each day to be still in a quiet place and meditate on the word of that day. Allow the Holy Spirit to speak to your heart, pay attention to what is being said, then respond accordingly. Do not rush the process, stay in the moment, and be blessed by God's presence. When you are praying the prayers included in the book, please know that each prayer is only a guide to get you started. Allow the Holy Spirit to move in you so that the prayers become personal to you, your families, and situation or circumstance that may be going on amongst you. The declarations are to be spoken with authority and power. Nothing happens until a word is spoken; God created the entire universe with the words that came out of his mouth, you have the power to do the same thing.

Remember that this is a 21-day challenge, do not do multiple days at once, and don't panic if you miss a day.

Just jump right back into it and **Make God A Habit!**

It is my prayer that your time with God will continue way beyond the 21 days. I pray that this challenge will make your prayer life and your time with God stronger and more exciting, starting each day looking forward to your time with God, enjoying him and allowing him to create in you a clean heart and a new spirit just as his word says in Psalm 51:10. You're going to be amazed at what God can and will do for you, through you and with you during those intimate times together.

God Bless and thank you for your support!

Deirdre Joyner

Make God A Habit
A
21-Day
Challenge

DAY

1

Scripture:

Be alert, be present, I'm about to do something brand-new. It's bursting out! Don't you see it? There it is! I'm making a road through the desert, rivers in the badlands. Isaiah 43:19 MSG

Behold, I am doing a new thing; now it springs forth, do you not perceive it? I will make a way in the wilderness and rivers in the desert. ESV

Prayer:

Lord I praise you for the new thing that you are doing in my life today. Thank you for new ideas, new money, new jobs, new opportunities, new relationships, new mindsets, and new ministries. Thank you for making a way when there seems to be no way. Thank you, Lord, for bringing me out the wilderness and thank you for watering the dry places of my life. As your doing these things for me Lord, I believe that you are also working on behalf of those attached to me. I receive the new thing right now Lord, in Jesus name, Amen.

Declaration:

I declare and decree that I receive the new thing that God is doing in my . . .

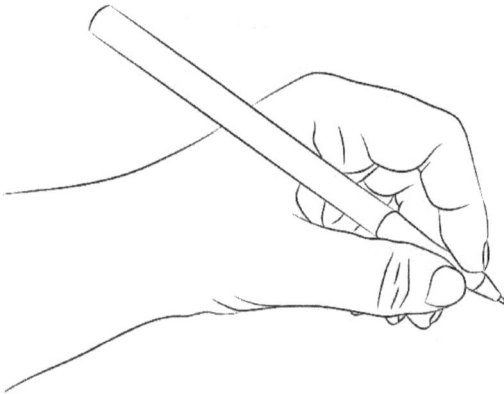

Journal:

Do you need a new thing to take place in your mind, body, health, finances? Do you need a new thing to take place in your family, your ministry or in your church?

● Whatever your needs are, write them down and speak the declaration over it.

_____

_____

_____

_____

_____

_____

_____

_____

_____

_____

_____

_____

_____

_____

_____

_____

Deirdre Joyner

_____

_____

_____

_____

_____

_____

_____

_____

_____

_____

_____

_____

_____

_____

_____

_____

_____

_____

_____

_____

_____

_____

_____

DAY

2

Scripture:

If you are willing and obedient, you will eat the good of the land. Isaiah 1:19 NIV

If you willingly obey, you'll feast like kings. MSG

Prayer:

Lord I thank you for your word! I thank you that there is a reward in obedience. Help me Lord to be obedient to your will and your ways today. When I stray please correct me and guide me in the way I shall go. Thank you, Lord, it is my heart's desire to please you and it cannot and will not happen without you. So, I ask you Lord to cleanse me, change me, and mold me. Lord, I also pray that you help my children, my nieces, nephews and all the young people of this generation to be obedient to your will and ways today. I stand in the gap for them today

Lord. In Jesus name, Amen

Declaration:

I declare and decree that I am willing and obedient and I will eat like a King!

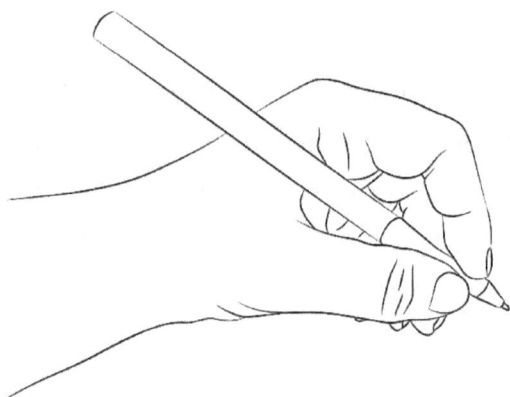

Journal:

We please God when we are obedient, there is a blessing in obedience. We must recognize and work on any area of disobedience.

• Where are you struggling with obedience? Write it down and declare that you are obedient in that area(s), keep declaring this until you are no longer struggling in that area(s).

_____

_____

_____

_____

_____

_____

_____

_____

_____

_____

_____

_____

_____

_____

_____

_____

_____

_____

_____

_____

_____

_____

_____

_____

_____

_____

_____

_____

_____

_____

_____

_____

_____

_____

_____

_____

_____

_____

_____

DAY

3

Scripture:

A blessing for you because the Lord your God loves you. Deuteronomy 23:5 KJV

Prayer: Father it is so wonderful to know that you love me and that you take care of me because of that love. I would be nothing without your love, I need your love today, I want your love today. I want your love for my children and my children's children. I want your love for my mother, my father, my sisters, my brothers, my aunts, my uncles. and all those that are connected in some way. Thank you for loving me and blessing me in this day Lord. In Jesus name I pray, Amen.

Declaration:

I declare and decree that the Lord my God loves me!

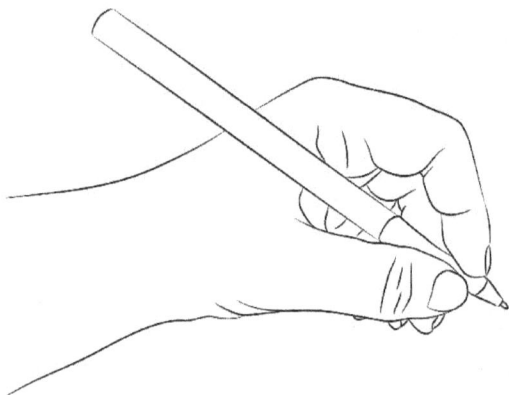

Journal:

Sometimes it's easier for people to believe something if they see it, therefore write down God loves me!

● Write this until you truly believe it; and for those who already believe it, write it so that you don't forget it!

_____

_____

DAY

4

Scripture:

Be angry and sin not: let not the sun go down upon your wrath. Ephesians 4:26 KJV

Go ahead and be angry. You do well to be angry but don't use your anger as a fuel for revenge. And don't stay angry. Don't go to bed angry. MSG

Prayer:

My Father in heaven, I know that anger is not a sin, Lord help me to not say or do mean and hateful things in the midst of my anger. Help me Lord to not allow anger to take residence in my heart. Help me to evict any deep-rooted anger. I do not want to be an angry person. Touch my heart Lord and help me to be a loving, peaceful and kind person. Thank you, in Jesus name I pray. Amen

Declaration:

I declare that anger has no control over me!

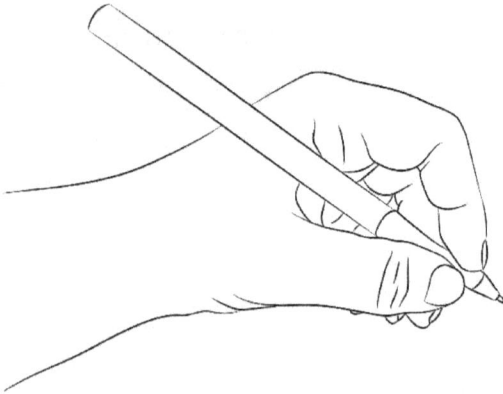

Journal:

We all have experienced anger. Anger itself is not a sin, anger is an emotion. If not dealt with correctly anger can lead you to do sinful things. We can say or do some really hurtful things in anger. On the flip side of that, people have become angry about many things and gave birth to some profound movements and causes.

● So, ask yourself, what makes you angry and how do you normally respond to that anger? Do you hold it in? Do you talk about it? Or do you lash out and become violent/aggressive?

If so, what are some alternative methods to manage your anger in a healthy way?

_____

_____

_____

_____

_____

_____

_____

_____

_____

_____

_____

_____

_____

_____

_____

_____

_____

_____

_____

_____

_____

_____

_____

_____

_____

_____

_____

_____

_____

_____

_____

_____

_____

_____

_____

_____

DAY

5

Scripture:

The desire of the slothful killeth him; for his hands refuse to labour. Proverbs 21:25 KJV

Lazy people finally die of hunger because they won't get up and go to work. Proverbs 21:25 MSG

Prayer:

Father thank you for waking me up this morning with a healthy mind and body. Help me Lord to put this mind and body to good use today. Help me to be productive, not only for myself but for my family, friends, church, community and anyone you put on my path today Lord. Remove anything or anyone that will hinder the productivity of my day. Thank you, in Jesus name I pray. Amen

Declaration:

I declare that today is a blessing and I will use it wisely!

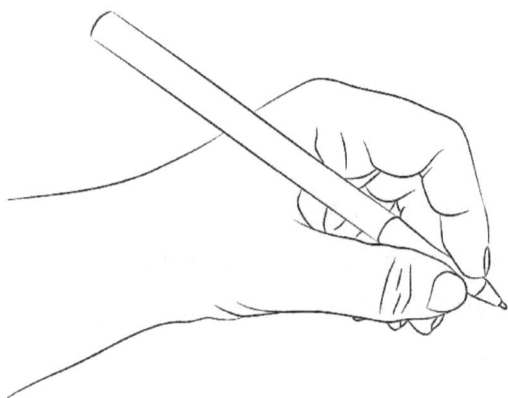

Journal:

We all have experienced times of laziness, but we cannot allow laziness to have control over us. God has blessed us all with gifts and talents to serve him and one another. As we use our gifts and talents, God blesses us with the ability to earn a living for ourselves so we can take care of our responsibilities and to also be able to bless others. Some may choose a traditional 9-5 while others may choose more creative options. No one way is better than the other, whatever works for the individual. Just use what God gave you and watch him bless the work of your hands.

● Are you a lazy person? If so, ask God to deliver you from it. Write down your gifts and talents then pray that God shows you how to use them.

_____
_____
_____
_____
_____
_____
_____
_____
_____

DAY

6

Scripture:

OH, taste and see that the Lord is good. Psalm 34:8 KJV

Prayer:

Lord I've tasted and I've seen that you are good. Thank you for your goodness. You were good to me when I didn't know you were there. You were good to me when I wasn't even good to myself. You brought me out the wilderness, you placed my feet on solid ground and you made my crooked paths straight. You blocked the hands of the enemy several times in my life. Lord I thank you that no weapon formed against me has ever prospered! Thank you, Jesus, for preserving me for such a time as now. Hallelujah and Amen!

Declaration:

I declare and decree that God will continue to overwhelm me with his goodness!

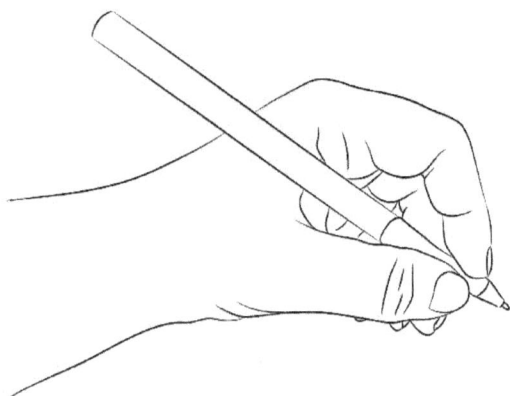

Journal:

God is good, even in the smallest things.

● In what ways, grand or small has God shown you his goodness? Write down everything that comes to you.

_____

_____

_____

_____

_____
_____
_____
_____
_____
_____
_____
_____
_____
_____
_____
_____
_____
_____
_____
_____
_____
_____
_____
_____
_____
_____
_____

_____

_____

_____

_____

_____

_____

_____

_____

_____

_____

_____

_____

_____

_____

_____

_____

_____

_____

_____

_____

_____

_____

_____

_____

DAY

7

Scripture:

The Lord is my shepherd, I shall not want.
Psalm 23:1 KJV

The Lord is my shepherd, I have all I need.
NLT

Prayer:

My father in heaven I thank you for being my shepherd. Lord I know that I am like a sheep and without you, I would wonder off and get lost. Thank you, Lord, for watching over me, guiding me, thank you for protecting me from danger, and providing all that I need. In Jesus name I pray Amen.

Declaration:

I declare and decree that the Lord will meet my every need!

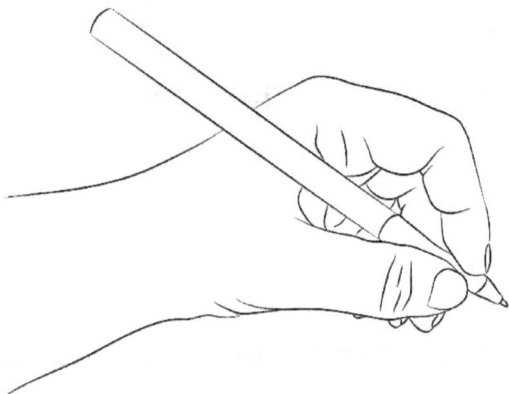

Journal:

What are the things that you want from God?

● Write them down. Then ask yourself why do you want these things, are they only useful for you or is it something that God can use to bless his people?

_____

_____

_____

_____

_____

_____

_____

_____

_____

_____

_____

_____

_____

_____

_____

_____

_____

_____

_____

_____

_____

_____

_____

_____

DAY

Scripture:

O give thanks unto the Lord for he is good, his mercy endures forever. Psalm 107:1 KJV

Prayer:

Lord I thank you for this day! I'm so thankful that today brings new mercy and new grace for me, my family and friends. We are blessed with another chance to get it right. As you bless us Lord with new mercy and new grace today, help us Lord to also extend that same mercy and grace to others. Thank you, Amen.

Declaration:

I declare that God's goodness and mercy are with me today!

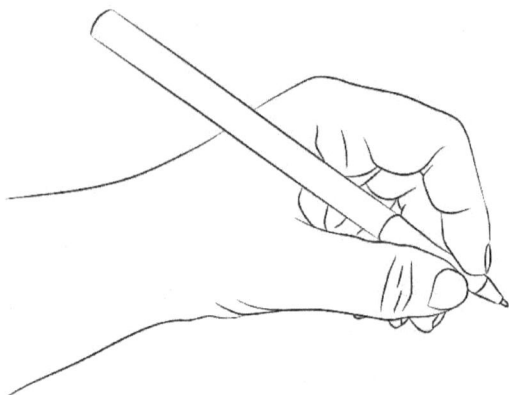

Journal:

The key to being blessed is to always remain grateful for the things that God has already done for you.

● Take 1 minute or less and write down 10 things that you're thankful for. Follow this simple format:

God I am thankful for. . .

_____

_____

_____

_____

_____

_____

_____

_____

_____

_____

_____

_____

_____

_____

_____

_____

_____

_____

_____

_____

_____

_____

_____

_____

_____
_____
_____
_____
_____
_____
_____
_____
_____
_____
_____
_____
_____
_____
_____
_____
_____
_____
_____
_____
_____
_____
_____

DAY

Scripture:

For I know the plans I have for you, declares the Lord. Plans to prosper you and to not harm you, plans to give you hope and a future. Jeremiah 29:11 NIV

Prayer:

Lord I thank you that there is hope for me, my family and my friends. I thank you for the plan of prosperity in our lives. Lord I ask you to not only prosper us financially, but to also prosper us mentally, physically, spiritually, and emotionally. Prosper us Lord in our relationships today, I call in divine connections. Help us all Lord to not only walk in prosperity but to first accept the fact that prosperity, peace and safety are all part of a life with you.

In Jesus name, Amen!

Declaration:

I declare and decree that the Lord has great plans for me!

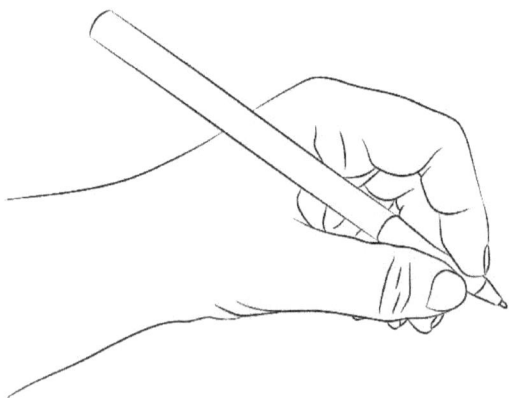

Journal:

What plans do you have for your life?

● Write them down then pray over them. Ask God to show you if your plans are or are not in alignment with the plans, he has for you. Make changes as the Holy Spirit leads you.

_____

_____

_____

_____

_____

_____

_____

_____

_____

_____

_____

_____

_____

_____

_____

_____

_____

_____

_____

_____

_____

_____

_____

_____

_____

_____

_____

_____

_____

_____

_____

_____

_____

_____

_____

_____

_____

_____

_____

_____

_____

_____

_____

_____

_____

_____

_____

_____

_____

_____

_____

_____

_____

_____

_____

_____

_____

_____

_____

_____

_____

_____

_____

_____

_____

_____

DAY

10

Scripture:

Trust in the Lord with all thine heart, and lean not unto your own understanding; in all thy ways acknowledge him, and he shall direct thy paths. Proverbs 3:5 KJV

Trust God from the bottom of your heart; don't try to figure out everything on your own. MSG

Prayer:

Lord I will trust you no matter what it looks like today. It may not look good, but I know that all things are working together for my good. I will put my hope in you and your word. I don't care what the doctor says, or what the bank says, Lord I don't even care what my family and friends say. Lord I know what your word says, and I trust you. Amen

Declaration:

I declare that I will not talk to God about how big my problems are, but I will talk to my problems about how big my God is!

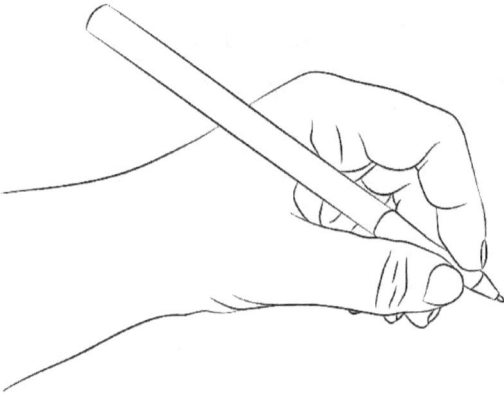

Journal:

Sometimes it is really hard to trust God, we look around and see ourselves surrounded by problems or situations of every kind. Most times these situations linger around for more time than we desire, so naturally we start to panic and try to figure out a plan to change our situation. This response most often makes matters worse in the long run.

● Do you really trust God, or do you take matters into your own hands? Examine your heart and write down your honest findings. No matter where you are with this, please stay in constant prayer.

_____

_____

_____

_____

_____

_____

_____

_____

_____

_____

_____

_____

_____

DAY

11

Scripture:

This is my commandment, That ye love one another, as I have loved you. John 15:12 KJV

Prayer:

Father I thank you for your love today. Thank you for loving me when I didn't even love myself. Thank you for loving me when I was unlovable. Lord you have blessed me with your love, so please help me to be an instrument of love today. Show me how to be more loving toward the people you put on my path today. Thank you in Jesus name. Amen

Declaration:

I declare that I am an instrument of love.

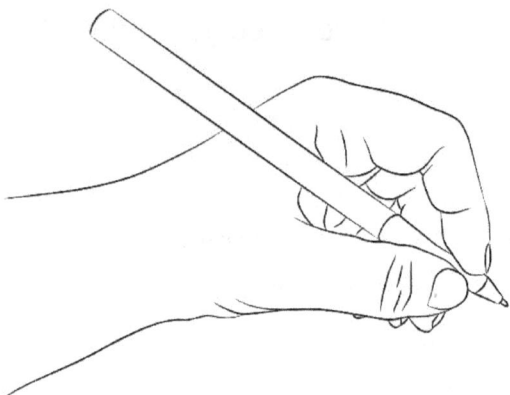

Journal:

God is love, so it is crucial that as believers that we exemplify love to others. We must not pick and choose who we love. We must love all God's people; no matter their age, race, gender, social or economic status. In other words, you shouldn't just love those that look like you, act like you or those that live near you. Love everyone!

● Are you a loving person? Do you discriminate against certain people, if so who and why? Examine your heart on this topic and write down everything that comes to you; good or bad. Then pray for God to keep your heart light with his love.

_____

_____

_____

_____

_____

_____

_____

_____

_____

_____

_____

_____

_____

_____

_____

_____

_____

_____

_____

_____

_____

_____

_____

_____

_____

_____

_____

_____

_____

_____

_____

_____

_____

_____

_____

_____

_____

_____

_____

_____

_____

DAY

12

Scripture:

And let us not be weary in well doing, for in due season we shall reap, if we faint not. Galatians 6:9 KJV

So let's not allow ourselves to get fatigued doing good. At the right time we will harvest a good crop if we don't give up or quit. MSG

Prayer:

Lord you know that it is really rough right now (on the job, in my finances, in my marriage, with the kids). I've been praying and believing that things will change soon. It seems like the more I pray, the worse things get. Lord I know that the enemy wants me to give up, I will not give up! I will continue to pray, I will hold on to you and your word. When my hands get tired of holding on, Lord I ask for you to please carry me through. Lord your word in Matthew 21:22 says that if I believe, I will receive everything I ask for in prayer. Lord I believe and I hold you to your word. Amen

Declaration:

I declare that I will not give up! I will not quit!

Journal:

Patiently waiting on God can be very

challenging at times. You put the work in as a believer by doing the things of God, you pray, praise, worship, read, fast, and give. In the midst of waiting we get discouraged because we don't see any obvious signs of change, at this point, it's easy to think that God has forgotten us. If this is how you're feeling today, please don't stop believing and doing the things of God! He hears and sees everything, he is working behind the scenes to bring you good in his time, in his way. He is an on-time God!

• Are you feeling weary today? If so what situation or circumstance are contributing to this current state? Write it down and speak over that situation out loud. Tell the situation that God is working on your behalf and that you will not give up.

_____
_____
_____
_____

_____

_____

_____

_____

_____

_____

_____

_____

_____

_____

_____

_____

_____

_____

_____

_____

_____

_____

_____

_____

_____

_____

DAY

13

Scripture:

If you stop your ears to the cries of the poor, your cries will go unanswered. Proverbs 21:13 MSG

Prayer:

Lord help me not to be selfish or inconsiderate towards others. Help me Lord to be a person that cares about the needs of those that are less fortunate than myself. Show me who to bless and how I can be a blessing to someone today. Open my eyes and ears so that I can easily spot an opportunity to bless others in any way that I can. I also ask that you touch my heart Lord and bless me with the spirit of generosity. Thank you, in Jesus name Amen.

Declaration:

I declare that I am blessed to be a blessing.

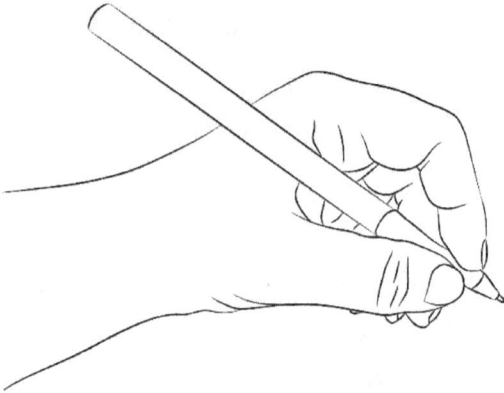

Journal:

God loves a cheerful giver. 2 Corinthians 9:7

Give and it shall be given to you. A good measure, pressed down, shaken together and running over, will be poured into your lap. For with the measure you use, it will be measured to you. Luke 6:30 NIV

Have you ever noticed that stingy or selfish people are always in the state of neediness?

They keep their hands closed tight to preserve what they have, they don't realize that closed hands don't leave room to receive. With God you must give in order to receive (give and it shall be given unto you).

• When was the last time you helped someone in anyway? It's not always about money, have you given someone a ride who does not have transportation? Have you offered a free service for someone in need? This can be anything from babysitting for a single mom or dad, or going to clean for an elderly friend/family member. Write down the most recent things you've done for someone. What is your heart saying about your generosity or stinginess?

_____

_____

_____

_____

_____

_____

_____

_____

_____

_____

_____

_____

_____

_____

_____

_____

_____

_____

_____

_____

_____

_____

_____

_____

_____

_____

_____

DAY

14

Scripture:

Death and life are in the power of the tongue, and they that love it shall eat the fruit thereof. Proverbs 18:21 KJV

Words kill, words give life; they're either poison or fruit- you choose. MSG

Prayer:

Father I thank you that I have the physical ability to speak today. Father help me to use my words to encourage, to build and to create life and life more abundantly. Father with your words, you created the entire world and everything in it. As your child, I have inherited that same trait and I need you to help me to use this trait as you would see fit. Thank you, in Jesus name I pray. Amen

Declaration:

I speak life, in all things, at all times!

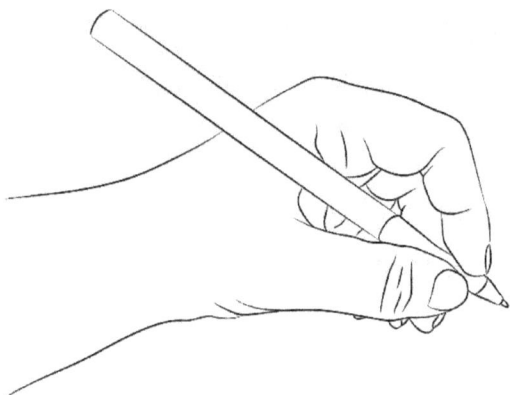

Journal:

We must be careful with the words that come out of our mouth. In relationships, our tongues can cause wounds that can last a lifetime. If we're not careful, our words can also block a fervent prayer. Sometimes we'll pray for something, then just as we finish praying, we say something negative. We pray for a financial breakthrough, then 5 minutes later we say, "Lord I don't know how

I'm going to pay these bills." Brothers and sisters, we must really be careful with guarding our tongues.

● Do you struggle with speaking negative things in the atmosphere? Do you block your own prayers? Or do you use your words to hurt people? Be honest with yourself, write down your struggle and pray for deliverance in this area.

_____

_____

_____

_____

_____

_____

_____

_____

_____

_____

_____

_____

_____

_____

_____

_____

_____

_____

_____

_____

_____

_____

_____

_____

_____

_____

_____

_____

_____

_____

_____

_____

_____

_____

_____

DAY

15

Scripture:

I can do all things through Christ which strengthens me. Philippians 4:13 KJV

Prayer:

Lord I thank you for your strength today! Strength to get out the bed this morning, strength to say my prayers, strength to exercise, strength to bathe and get dressed, strength to go to work, and Lord I thank you for the strength to face todays issues and challenges. Thank you for empowering me today. Amen.

Declaration: I declare and decree that I can do all things through Christ which strengthens me!

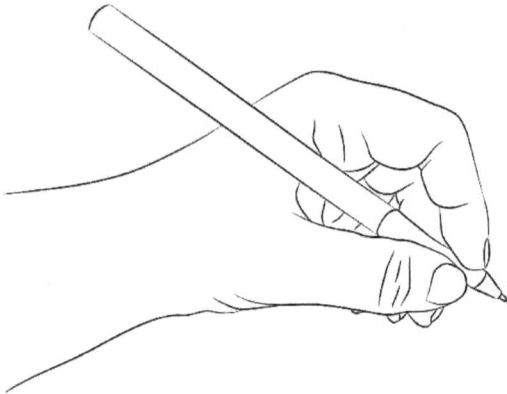

Journal:

There are different levels of strength needed. Needing strength to get up and go to work, is very different from needing the strength to get through a divorce, the death of a parent, or a medical crisis. I don't know what type of strength you need today, but it is available through Christ Jesus.

● Where are you lacking strength right now

in this moment? Write it down and speak the declaration/scripture over it. Do this everyday until you feel strength rising up within you.

_____

_____

_____

_____

_____

_____

_____

_____

_____

_____

_____

_____

_____

_____

_____

_____

_____

_____

_____

_____

_____

_____

_____

_____

_____

_____

_____

_____

_____

_____

_____

_____

_____

_____

_____

_____

_____

_____

_____

_____

_____

_____

_____

_____

_____

_____

_____

_____

_____

_____

_____

_____

_____

_____

_____

_____

_____

_____

_____

_____

_____

_____

_____

_____

DAY

16

Scripture:

The rich ruleth over the poor, and the borrower is servant to the lender. Proverbs 22:7 KJV

The poor are always ruled over by the rich, so don't borrow and put yourself under their power. MSG

Prayer:

Lord I thank you for all that I have. Help me to be a good steward over what you have given me. Help me to spend wisely, being very careful not to spend unnecessarily and to not over spend. Father help me to be a lender and not a borrower. I rebuke financial bondage in the name of Jesus! With this prayer, I command every financial mountain to be removed from me and to be cast into the sea. Get thee behind me Satan in the mighty name of Jesus! Your word in Deuteronomy 15:6 says that I shall lend to many nations and shall not borrow. Help me to do my part so that your word comes to path in my life. Help me to leave a legacy of financial freedom for my children's children, children. In Jesus name, Amen!

Declaration:

I declare and decree that I am a lender not a borrower!

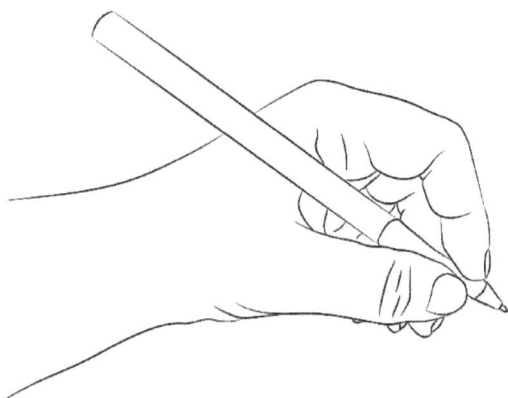

Journal:

We were never created to be in debt, or in

any form of financial bondage. Therefore, we must constantly seek God's financial guidance. Go to him in prayer about your financial decisions. Be a good steward over what he has given you. In other words, don't be wasteful, don't overspend, be a generous giver and pay off any debts you owe. If you have a bill, pay it and pay it on time. I understand that situations come up sometimes, just make the appropriate arrangements with the other party. Never enter an agreement with the intent of not paying the bill. As God's children, we are to keep our word. Don't block your blessings!

● Do you have unnecessary debt? Are you an over spender? Are you constantly getting over on creditors, promising to pay but have no means or intentions of doing so? Search your heart on this matter.

_____

_____

_____

_____
_____
_____
_____
_____
_____
_____
_____
_____
_____
_____
_____
_____
_____
_____
_____
_____
_____
_____
_____
_____

DAY

17

Scripture:

But I will restore you to health and heal your wounds declares the Lord, because you are called an outcast, Zion for whom no one cares. Jeremiah 30:17 NIV

As for you, I'll come with healing, curing the incurable, because they all gave up on you and dismissed you as hopeless- that good-for-nothing Zion. MSG

Prayer:

Lord I thank you for this day. Lord I'm praying for healing today in my body. Lord lay your healing hands all over my_____. I rebuke sickness of every form, known and unknown. Lord I command every member of my body to operate exactly how you created it to. I will not be bound by any sickness or physical limitation. The devil is a liar! And Lord, I ask that you also bless my family and my friends in their bodies today. Lord give them the healing that they need. I ask you to heal cancer, lupus, glaucoma, diabetes, epilepsy, arthritis, aneurysms, addictions, depression and all other forms of mental illness, heart conditions, asthma, and any other sickness and infirmity that was sent from hell. Thank you, Lord, I receive the healing in Jesus name. Amen

Declaration: I declare that I am healed! I am whole!

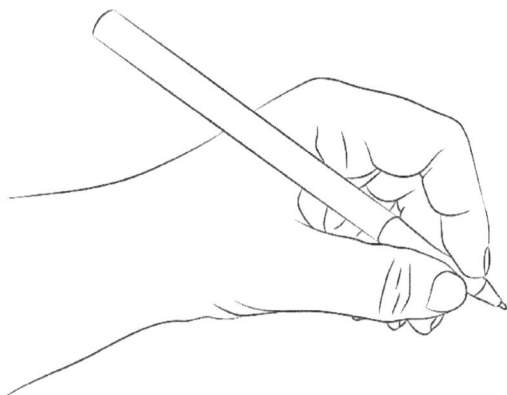

Journal:

Serving God and mankind can be very difficult if we are plagued with sickness and or disease. Please know that this is not the will of God. There's work to be done for the Kingdom of God and it cannot be done to the fullest with bound up bodies. Recently the enemy tried to attack my speech, my mouth was twisted and my speech became slurred. It was very difficult to speak, but I refused to let that stop me from giving God praise with my mouth. I used that same mouth and told the devil that he's a liar and he cannot have my words, "I need my words to speak life and to move mountains." It was a daily struggle, But God blessed me and renewed my speech. Hallelujah!

● Are you faced with a sickness today? Don't give up! Let the enemy know that sickness is not an option!

Write down the sickness and speak to that sickness daily . . . I am healed! I am whole!

_____

_____

_____

_____

_____

_____

_____

_____

_____

_____

_____

_____

_____

_____

_____

_____

_____

_____

_____

_____

_____

_____

_____

_____

_____

_____

_____

_____

_____

_____

_____

_____

_____

_____

_____

_____

_____

_____

_____

_____

_____

_____

_____

_____

_____

_____

_____

_____

_____

_____

_____

_____

Deirdre Joyner

144

DAY

18

Scripture:

You are altogether beautiful, my darling; there is no flaw in you. Song of Solomon 4:7 NIV

You're beautiful from head to toe, my dear love, beautiful beyond compare, absolutely flawless. MSG

Prayer:

Lord I thank you that I am fearfully and wonderfully made. There were times when I struggled with accepting this. I thank you for helping me to finally embrace the fact that you made me exactly the way you needed and wanted me to be. My personality, my outer appearance, my dreams, and my DNA are all part of the perfect plan you have for me. Help me to always remember this, leaving no room to compare myself with others in anyway. Thank you, Lord, for creating me in your image, in Jesus name I pray. Amen

Declaration: I am BEAUTIFUL!

Journal:

We live in a time where's body image is everything for millions of people from all over the world. Cosmetic surgery has reached an all time high. People are so focused on changing their outer appearance so that they will look "perfect", not knowing and accepting the fact that God has already made them perfect. There is nothing wrong with wanting to look good and to be beautiful, but let's not forget that beauty is within. You can spend millions of dollars on liposuction, nose jobs, tummy tucks etc., but what difference would it make if your mean, angry, stingy and unloving on the inside? God is more concerned with our minds and the issue of our hearts, so let's focus on our inner beauty and take care of the wonderful bodies that God has given us.

● Are you happy with the way God made you? Or are you always wishing that you were taller, shorter, lighter, darker, prettier, smarter? Be honest with yourself and write down everything that you wish you could change with your outer appearance. Wake up each morning, look in the mirror and say, "I am BEAUTIFUL!"

DAY

19

Scripture:

For if you forgive other people when they sin against you, your heavenly Father will also forgive you. But if you do not forgive others their sins, your Father will not forgive your sins. Matthew 6:14-15 NIV

Prayer:

Lord I thank you that you are a forgiving God. Each day with you brings new forgiveness, canceling out the previous day's sins, failures and mistakes. Lord I pray that you help me to become more like you in this area today. Removing any known or unknown unforgiveness. Clothe me Lord with the spirit of forgiveness, I receive it right now in your son Jesus name. Amen

Declaration: I am forgiving!

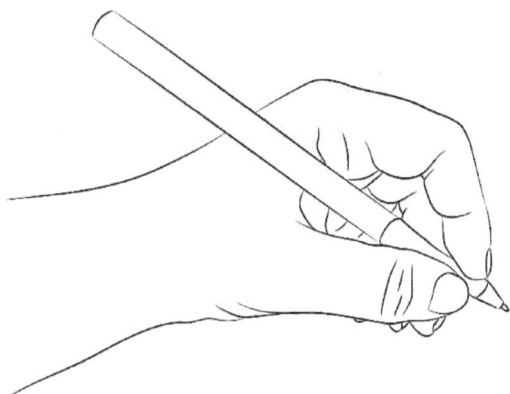

Journal:

Forgiveness is not an option, it's a commandment from our Heavenly Father. The word says that IF we forgive others, THEN our Heavenly Father will forgive us (Matthew 6:14-15) Lord knows that I am only human and I'm always in need of The Lord's forgiveness. If forgiving others is the condition for receiving forgiveness for my sins, then forgiving others is what I'll do. I'm not saying that it'll be easy, but it has to be done!

● Are you holding on to any unforgiveness today? If so, what is it and with whom? Search your heart, write down your findings and pray over the situation. Remember forgiveness is for you, not the offender. Forgiveness sets you free from the bondage of unforgiveness, bitterness, and hate.

_____

_____

_____

_____

_____

_____

_____

_____

_____

_____

_____

_____

DAY

20

Scripture:

Say to those with fearful hearts, "Be strong, do not fear; your God will come, he will come with vengeance; with divine retribution he will come and save you. Isaiah 35:4 NIV

Tell fearful souls, "Courage! Take heart! God is here, right here, on his way to put things right and redress all wrongs. He's on his way! He'll save you!" MSG

Prayer:

Lord I know that you did not give me the spirit of fear, but right now in this moment I'm feeling fearful. I'm feeling fear about-
_____. Lord in Psalm 56:3 David said when he was afraid, he trusted you. Help me to be more like David today, trusting and believing in you, your word, and your power. Lord, I'm trusting that you will remove this fear from me, replacing it with faith and the calming peace that comes with it. Thank you Lord, I

receive the gift of faith today in Jesus name. Amen

Declaration:

I declare and decree that I am not afraid!

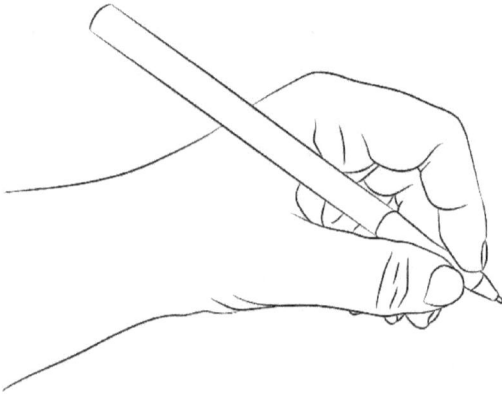

Journal:

It is impossible for fear and faith to exist at the same time. Either your trusting and believing God in that moment or you're not.

God knows that we will sometimes struggle with fear, that's why scripture says, "fear not, I am with you" (Isaiah 41:10). As believers, we must know God's word. Faith comes by hearing and hearing by the word of God (Romans 10:17). Therefore; if you want a deeper and stronger faith, you must spend time reading, hearing, and meditating on God's word. This is the only way to conquer fear! You must know what God says about you and your situation!

● Write down your fear(s), then search out what God says about that situation. Write the scripture down next to the fear, meditate on that scripture until fear scatters and faith arises!

_____

_____

_____

_____

_____

_____

_____

_____

_____

_____

_____

_____

_____

_____

_____

_____

_____

_____

_____

_____

_____

_____

_____

_____

_____

_____

_____

_____

_____

DAY

21

Scripture:

Weeping may endure for a night, but joy cometh in the morning. Psalm 30:5 KJV

The nights of crying your eyes out give way to days of laughter. MSG

Prayer:

My good good Father in heaven, I am so thankful that the season of weeping has been cast away from me. Lord you know that I have wept for many years; I wept as a struggling single mother, I wept about the kids, I wept about the marriage, the divorce. Lord I wept about the abuse, the betrayal, I wept about the death of loved ones, and I wept about the medical condition. Lord I have had my share of weeping, but today I rejoice in this beautiful season of Joy! Thank you, Father, for the joy, peace, happiness, laughter and wholeness that I have today. Lord I pray that it'll last forever and ever!

Father my heart goes out to every man,

Deirdre Joyner

woman, and child who may be in their weeping season today. God bless them in Jesus mighty name. Give them the strength and the faith to endure. Lord if my testimony can uplift and bring hope to anyone today then send them my way. I promise to prove your word true. In Jesus name. Amen

Journal:

Weeping may endure for a night! But joy comes in the morning! Psalm 30:5

176

There are many scriptures that I consider as my favorites, but this scripture here is truly part of my life's testimony. At 45 years old I've definitely had my fair share of heartbreaks, disappointments, and sorrows. As a new and immature believer, I use to think that this scripture meant that my weeping would literally be over the next day. I remember being so depressed at times, rushing to get to bed because in my mind it'll all be over when I wake up in the morning. It took many sermons and growth through trials and situations before I really understood this scripture.

Weeping for a night is basically a season of darkness, or testing. No one knows how long this season will last, some seasons of weeping are much longer than others. These are the times when it's crucial to keep our eyes on God, trusting and believing in him more than ever. In these times God is doing a great work in you and for you, he is working on a master plan. Trust me, it'll be worth it in the end. There is a great reward in trusting

God! At the appointed time God will show up, he will restore you with joy and peace. He will repay you for what you've been through, and when he shows up, trust me he will always show out! Doing and giving more than we could've ever imagined.

● The journal activity today is to just sit back, close your eyes and take it all in. Meditate on God and his word for a few moments. Think about how God has showed out for you before, and let that be your peace in knowing that God is about to show out again. He's about to do something so awesome for you and your family! Get Ready! Get Ready! Get Ready!

God Bless and Peace be with you!

Deirdre

_____

_____

_____

_____
_____
_____
_____
_____
_____
_____
_____
_____
_____
_____
_____
_____
_____
_____
_____
_____
_____
_____
_____
_____
_____

www.ingramcontent.com/pod-product-compliance
Lightning Source LLC
Chambersburg PA
CBHW071338090426
42738CB00012B/2930